# THE SMOKER'S ADDICTIONARY

*Roslyn Schwartz*

A Lucy-Caroll Book

**Linden Press/Simon & Schuster**
New York 1985

Published by Linden Press/Simon & Schuster
A Division of Simon & Schuster, Inc.
Simon & Schuster Building
Rockefeller Center
1230 Avenue of the Americas
New York, New York 10020

LINDEN PRESS/SIMON & SCHUSTER and colophon
are trademarks of Simon & Schuster, Inc.

*Created and produced by*
Lucy-Caroll Limited
228 Gerrard Street East
Toronto, Ontario
Canada

Designed by Nancy Ruth Jackson
Edited by Beverley Endersby
Manufactured in Canada by D. W. Friesen

1 2 3 4 5 6 7 8 9 10

ISBN: 0-671-54400-4

## For Ma

I would like to extend a heartfelt thank you to all the people who helped me compile this dictionary: friends who thought they were being invited for dinner and discovered that the table was set with pencils and paper and family who by now know better than to think anything at all. I am also most grateful for the professional support of Beverley Endersby (smoker) and Carolyn Brunton (non-smoker) without fume none of this would have been possible. Thank you.

I was in the seventeenth hour of my umpteenth attempt over the past three years to finally, once and for all, give up smoking. Carrying myself carefully past places that sell cigarettes, I was walking to the subway when I noticed that everyone, absolutely everyone, including his/her dog, was smoking; even babies and toddlers looked as if they had just put one out. I had been following the How-to-Quit guides, kits, and pamphlets to the last gallon of orange juice; I was enrolled in an exercise class, took lots of showers, and never let go of my knitting unless it was to crunch on a carrot. But nothing had prepared me for this spectacle. I started to laugh—a wheezy sound grown rusty from disuse. Surely, I thought, smoking is too ghastly a subject to treat seriously all the time? And that was the beginning of this book. I hope it gives you some measure of comic relief and encouragement to attain your goal, whatever that might be.

# A

**abstinence** *(n)* Makes the heart grow stronger.

**acupuncture** *(n)* Suffering pins and needles for an outrageous fortune.

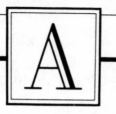

**addict** *(n)* One who would gladly face a firing squad for a cigarette.

**addiction** *(n)* Never having to say you've quit.

**addictionary** *(n)* A humorous, alphabetically arranged smoker's lexicon that can't be put down.

**alibi** *(n)* The dog you got so you could explain those midnight trips to the variety store.

**appetite** (*n*) Smoker's: No gain without pain. Non-smoker's: No pain without gain.

**ash** (n) The remains of a heavy smoker.

**ashtray** (n) Smoker's: The first thing one looks for in a stranger's house. Non-smoker's: A place to keep loose change.

**atmosphere** (n) The air that hovers over a dinner party of six people, one of whom is smoking.

**aversion therapy** (n) The "pig-out, freak-out, butt-out" school of quitting.

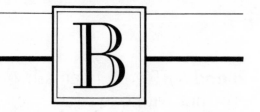

**bad taste** *(n)* Extinguishing cigarettes in half-empty cups of coffee or plates of food.

**bar-b-que** *(n)* Having your smoke and eating it too.

**blackholes** *(n)* Charred circles of mysterious origin found in clothing and carpeting.

**blackmail** *(n)* The price of cigarettes.

**blend** *(v)* To rub fallen ash into the carpet with one's foot.

**bogart** *(v)* "You just put your lips together—and *blow*."

**born again** *(adj)* Seeing the light when you need one.

**brand** (*n*) The distinctive mark on two fingers of the smoking hand that announces membership in a secret society.

**break** (*n*) The pause that depresses.

**breathless** *(n)* The title of
a film by Jean-Luc Godard
before the abolition of
smoking loges.

**bronchitis** *(n)* **1)** What a smoker would describe as a mild cough; **2)** Acute or chronic inflammation of the bronchial tubes of SOMEONE ELSE.

**bum** *(v)* To selflessly help one's friends cut down.

**butt** *(n)* A very short cigarette for a very hard-up smoker.

**bylaw** *(n)* The rule stating that meals will be served and public transport will arrive promptly upon lighting up.

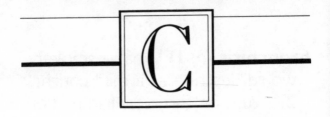

**cancer** *(n)* The fourth sign of the zodiac.

**carrot stick** *(n)* Hard to keep lit. . . .

**celery stick** *(n)* . . . even harder.

**chain smoking** *(n)* Never having to carry matches. *See also* joint.

**chewing tobacco** *(n)* Smoking without inhaling.

**cigar** *(n)* **1)** A device to keep people at harm's length; **2)** Smoldering aggression.

**cigarette** *(n)* **1)** The first-cigarette-of-the-day cigarette; **2)** The morning-coffee cigarette; **3)** The on-the-way-to-work cigarette; **4)** The "Let's get in a good morning's work" cigarette; **5)** The "How will I ever make it until lunch?" cigarette; **6)** The coffee-break cigarette; **7)** The telephone cigarette; **8)** The "Hang on while I get a cigarette" cigarette.

**9)** The "Where shall we go for lunch?" cigarette; **10)** The after-lunch cigarette; **11)** The "Let's get

in a good
afternoon's
work''
cigarette;
**12)** The
''How will I
ever make it
until five?''
cigarette;

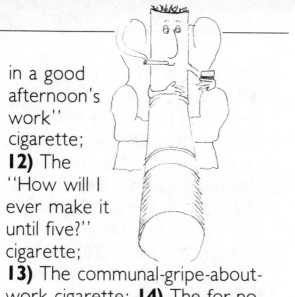

**13)** The communal-gripe-about-work cigarette; **14)** The for-no-particular-reason-at-all cigarette;
**15)** The ''How will I ever get all this work done?'' cigarette;
**16)** The ''Oh, I seem to already have one going'' cigarette; **17)** The almost-time-to-go cigarette;
**18)** The traveling-home cigarette;
**19)** The ''How nice to be home. I

think I'll just relax a bit" cigarette;
**20)** The pre-dinner drink 'n' chat cigarette; **21)** The making-the-salad cigarette; **22)** The between-courses cigarette; **23)** The dessert-and-coffee cigarette; **24)** The watching-TV cigarette; **25)** The "This is the worst program I've ever seen" cigarette; **26)** The one-last-cigarette-before-bed cigarette; **27)** The "Did the earth move for you?" cigarette; **28)** The "Why are you asking, weren't you there?" cigarette.

**cigarette holder** (*n*) A large butler named Jeeves.

**cocktail cigarettes** (n) Visual aids

**coffee** (n) One of the perks of
   smoking.

**cold turkey** (n) One who keeps
   cigarettes in the fridge.

**cough** (v) To exercise
   one's lungs
   before or
   after lighting
   up. (n) A
   signal to let
   one's loved
   ones know
   one is still
   around.

**crave** *(n)* An uncontrollable desire to smoke a cigarette, most intensely felt immediately after seriously contemplating quitting.

**cutting down** *(v)* Smoking less and enjoying it less.

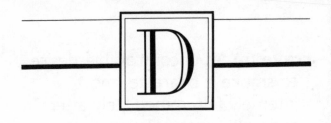

# D

**decision** *(n)* A firm commitment to put things off a little longer.

**deluxe** *(adj)* A big pack attack.

**dependence** *(n)* A smoker's offspring.

**disaster** *(n)* Cigarettes, women, and children first.

**diet** *(v)* To smoke only low-tar brands.

**discrimination** *(n)* Classified ads specifying beautiful, intelligent, non-smokers.

**disease** *(n)* See bronchitis, emphysema, heart attack, lung cancer. Better still, see your doctor.

**divorce** (n) The side effect of one partner's trying to quit.

**"Do you mind if I smoke?"** (trans.) "Why do all the ashtrays have lids on them?"

**drag** *(n)* Leaving your cigarettes in the pocket of his dress.

**drink** *(n)* Something for the other hand.

**drug** *(n)* Anything you do more than once.

# E

**emphysema** *(n)* A destructive complication of SOMEONE ELSE'S chronic bronchitis.

**environmental control** (*n*)
Going only to places such as libraries, theaters, swimming pools or department stores where one can't smoke.

**etiquette** (*n*) The code of behavior that says that polite society no longer requires a smoker to offer his/her pack to others before lighting up. Indeed, polite society no longer requires smokers.

**euphemism** *(n)*
SOMEONE ELSE.

**euphoria** *(n)*
Finding a
cigarette in the
corner of the
crumpled pack
you were sure
was empty,
especially at
3:00 A.M.

**excuses** *(n)* For smoking: **1)** I like to look busy; **2)** I have just been given a charming lighter; **3)** I hate myself anyway. For not smoking: none.

**exercise** *(n)* Trendy activity for ex-smokers. *See also* Cough.

**exhale** *(v)* To eliminate oxygen from the lungs to make room for cigarette tars and nicotine.

**ex-smoker** *(n)* A person who has not smoked for seven years, three months, five weeks, four days, six hours, one minute, and twenty-eight seconds.

**extra mild** *(adj)* **1)** Gasping at thin air; **2)** Something to smoke between cigarettes.

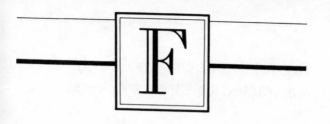

**fable** *(n)* Uncle George smoked two packs a day all his life and lived to the ripe old age of 112.

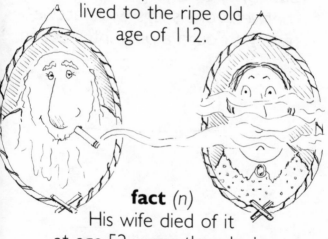

**fact** *(n)*
His wife died of it at age 52, even though she didn't smoke.

**fag** *(n)* A smoker who's only attracted to other smokers.

**fantasy** *(n)* A safe cigarette.

**fear** *(n)* **1)** Dropping a lit cigarette between one's legs while accelerating through a busy intersection;

**2)** Leaving a cigarette burning somewhere and not remembering where.

**filter** (n) The wasted half-inch of a cigarette.

**filthy habit** (n) A nun/smoker.

**fire** (n) The cry that follows the use of the wastepaper basket as an ashtray.

**flick** (n) A puff-and-snuff movie.

**foolproof** (adj) "How to take up smoking in ten days or your money back."

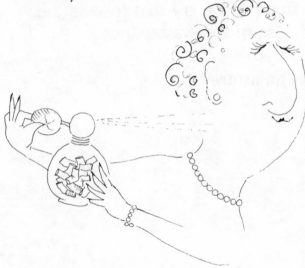

**fragrance** (n) The attar of stale ashtray worn by most smokers.

**french inhaling** *(v)* Depilatory smoking to remove unsightly nose hair.

**friends** *(n)* **1)** Those who offer one moral support and advice; **2)** Those who offer one cigarettes.

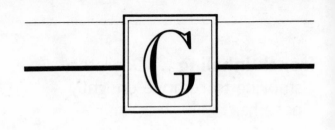

**gag** *(n)* A good joke told just as one is in the act of inhaling.

**G.A.S.P.** Acronym for Groups Against Smoking Persons.

**Gauloises** (*n*)
An affordable
alternative to
a weekend
in Paris.

**giving up** *(n)* "To cease smoking is the easiest thing I ever did; I ought to know because I've done it a thousand times." (Mark Twain)

**guilt** *(n)* The gold band round the filter of an expensive cigarette.

**gum** *(n)* Spearmint, sugarless, and now new yummy nicotine-flavor (by prescription only).

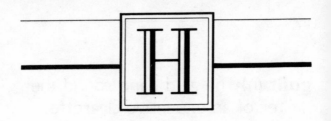

**habit** *(n)* A series of amazing coincidences.

**halitosis** *(n)* Breath that smells as bad as it tastes.

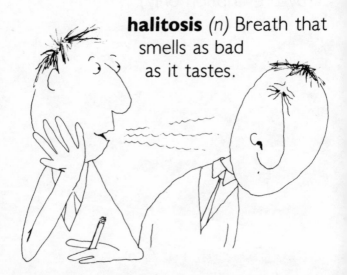

**Havana** (n) A city slightly south of Nirvana.

**health hazard** (n) Taking a lit cigarette away from a smoker.

**heart attack** (n) An unlucky strike.

**heavy smoker** (n) Someone who weighs 98 pounds.

**herbal cigarette** (n) Manually operated incense.

**highschool washrooms** (n) Training centers for the adolescent smoker.

**hookah** *(n)* Humidified smoke for asthmatics and/or snorkelers.

**hooked** *(adj)* Fishing a butt out of an overflowing ashtray.

**hypnosis** *(n)* An induced state re-sembling sleep brought on by listening to testimonials of recently reformed smokers.

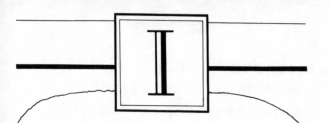

**"I'm cutting down."** *(trans.)* "I sleep three hours more a day."

**"I don't inhale."** *(trans.)* "I'm a pathological liar."

**"I'll just have one more before I leave."** *(trans.)* "Do you have a guest room?"

**"I'm trying to quit."** *(trans.)* "This gun is loaded."

**"I'm under a lot of stress right now."** *(trans.)* "I said, *I'm under a lot of stress right now.*"

**incentive** *(n)* To quit: **1)** Add years to your life; **2)** Reduce the risk of heart disease, bronchitis, emphysema and lung cancer; **3)** Save money; **4)** Improve the taste of food; **5)** End cigarette breath; **6)** Freshen up clothes, hair, and house; **7)** Improve stamina; **8)** Lose your smoker's hack. To smoke: mosquito control.

**inhale** *(v)* To draw deeply, like Picasso.

**insomnia** *(n)* Lying awake at night counting camels.

**insurance** *(n)* Buying by the carton.

**irony** *(n)* A non-smoker who dies of lung cancer.

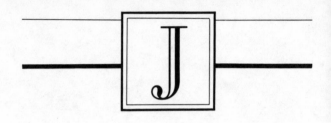

**jogging** *(n)* Running out for cigarettes.

**joint** *(n)* An illegal cigarette.

**joke** *(n)* Q: "Do you smoke after sex?" A: "I don't know, I've never looked."

**jungle mouth** *(n)*
Frond memories
of the night
before.

**kick** *(n)* The hit, rush or buzz you get . . . *(v)* to give up.

**king size** *(adj)* The moans of a recent ex-smoker.

**kissing** *(n)* The second most pleasant oral activity.

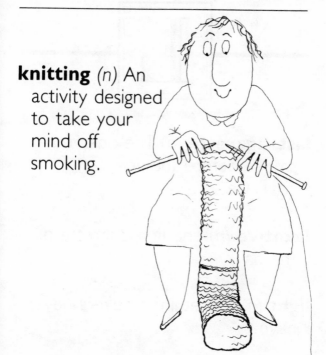

**knitting** *(n)* An activity designed to take your mind off smoking.

**Koop, C. Everett** *(n)* The man in the U.S.A. who determines that cigarette smoking is hazardous to your health. *See also* Surgeon General.

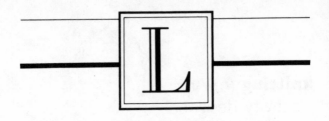

**last cigarette** *(n)* The one you smoke before the very last cigarette.

**laxative** *(n)* The first cigarette of the day.

**light** *(n)* Something smokers never have.

**lightbulb** *(n)* Q: "How many smokers does it take to change a lightbulb?" A: "Two. One to find a bulb and one to find a light."

**lighter** *(n)* Generic name for a candle, a toaster, a stove, and the cigarette one just finished smoking.

**lip print** *(n)* Method devised by female smokers, primarily, to check the condition of their lipstick.

**lobby** *(n)* Group of smokers in the hallway of a no-smoking public building.

**lox** *(n)* A salmon who lost the up-stream battle to quit.

**lung cancer** *(n)* A pathological condition characterized by an enlarged, tumor-like growth located in the respiratory organs of SOMEONE ELSE.

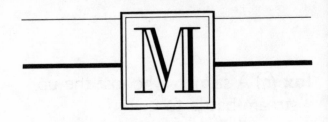

# M

**marijuana** *(n)* The socially acceptable cigarette.

**Marlboro Country** *(n)* Never, never, land.

**masochist** *(n)* A smoker who enjoys it.

**matchbook** *(n)* A small cardboard folder containing one damp paper match and an illegible phone number.

**menthol cigarettes** *(n)* A refreshing alternative to brushing your teeth.

---

**moral majority** *(n)* Non-smokers.

**mouthwash** *(n)* Bleach.

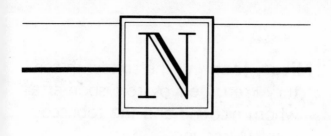

**nails** *(n)* Finger food.

**neurotic** *(adj)* One who brushes his/her tongue after every cigarette and smokes only one from each pack bought.

**Nicot, Jean** *(n)* The sixteenth-century French envoy to Lisbon after whom nicotine and the tobacco plant (*Nicotiana tabacum*) are named. It could be worse. He might have been called Hzorjsky.

Nicotina Tabacum

**nicotine** *(n)*
   **1)** Last year's decorator color;
   **2)** A heavy smoker between 12 and 20 years of age.

**nightmare** *(n)* Day 366 of one's stop-smoking program.

**non-smoker** *(n)* A terminal drag.

**nuclear holocaust** *(n)* A drastic, as yet untried, method for the global elimination of cigar smokers.

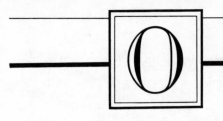

**office cigarette machine** *(n)*
Change smoking.

**opium** *(n)* A pipe dream.

**O.P.'s** *(n)* Other People's, a very popular brand among ex-smokers.

**oral fixation** *(n)* Worrying about bad breath when one may be suffering from heart disease.

**orgasm** *(n)* Smokers' foreplay.

**oxygen** *(n)* Something one seeks in which to enjoy a cigarette when it's too smoky at a party.

**oxymoron** *(n)* ''Avoid inhaling.''

**"oy vay"** *(trans.)* ''Go on, light another one, kill yourself, see if I care.''

# P

**pack** *(n)*
A bicep
extender

**passive smoking** *(n)* Choosing
the seat in front of the last seat
in the smoking section.

**Pavlovian response** *(n)* Smoking when the phone rings.

**peanuts** *(n)* Like cigarettes, it's hard to have just one.

**peer pressure** *(n)* The glaring looks of one's non-smoking contemporaries as one asks for an ashtray.

**peppermints** *(n)* A smokescreen.

**perseverence** *(n)* Lighting a cigarette off the electric stove.

**phlegm** *(n)* A pleasant-tasting, attractively colored, natural lubricant found in a variety of shapes and locations.

**piles** *(n)* Little mounds of butts found in parking lots.

**pink** *(adj)* A healthy lung.

**pipe** *(n)* An adult lollipop.

**pleasure** *(n)* ''A cigarette is the perfect type of a perfect pleasure. It is exquisite, and it leaves one unsatisfied. What more can one want?'' (Oscar Wilde)

**puff** *(n)* The magic drag-on.

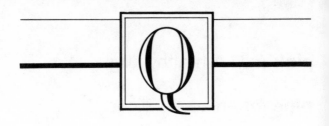

**quiche** *(n)* A savory flan eaten with spinach salad, typically order- ed while seated in designated non- smoking areas of chi-chi poo-poo restaurants by diners of ambi- guous gender.

**quickie** *(n)* A one-light stand.

**quit** *(v)* To finally stop buying ciga- rettes and apologetically begin to smoke everyone else's.

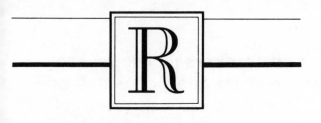

# R

**Raleigh, Sir Walter** *(n)* A famous Elizabethan trafficker in noxious substances.

**rationing** *(n)* Allowing oneself three, maybe five, well perhaps ten cigarettes a day, then smoking tomorrow's on credit.

**real smokers** (n) People who break the filters off with their teeth and carry engraved gold lighters.

**reality** (n) ". . . a crutch for people who can't deal with drugs." (Lily Tomlin)

**record** (n) Jim Purol and Mike Papa, smoking 135 cigarettes at a time. (*Guiness Book of World Records*)

**recycling** (n) Recovering the half-empty pack one spontaneously threw in the garbage the night before.

**regular** *(adj)* Cream, sugar, and five cigarettes.

**relapse** *(n)* The draw that broke the camel's pack.

**resolution** *(n)* Inevitably the first thing to go up in smoke on New Year's Day.

**resources** *(n)* Usually "inner" and "hidden"; like matches they are never there when one needs them.

**rhythm method** *(n)* Smoking only on one's safe days.

**risk** *(n)* What SOMEONE ELSE takes.

**ritual** *(n)* Deciding to quit once and for all.

**roll-your-own** *(n)* A typical "me generation" response.

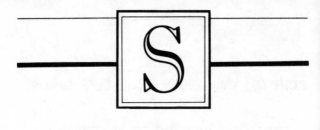

**second-hand smoke** (*n*) Can get right up your nose, if you're lucky.

**smoke-rings** *(n)* Items exchanged during any serious engagement.

**smoker** *(n)* An endangered species.

**smoking** *(n)* **1)** "A custom loathsome to the eye, hateful to the nose, harmful to the brain, dangerous to the lungs, and in the black, stinking fume thereof, nearest resembling the horrible Stygian smoke of the pit that is bottomless" (James I of England); **2)** "Smoking is fun. Smoking is cool. Smoking is, as far as I am concerned, the entire point of being an adult. It makes growing up genuinely worthwhile." (Fran Lebowitz)

**snack** *(v)* To eat compulsively between cigarettes.

**St. Blaise** *(n)* Patron saint of smokers.

**statistics** *(n)* It has been proven that smoking is one of the leading causes of statistics.

**stubb** *(n)* The only link between cigarettes and big toes.

**suicide** (*n*)
Kicking the
habit.

**surgeon general** (*n*) Nag, nag, nag.

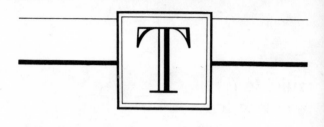

**tar** *(n)* Paves the way to
emphysema.

**tariff** *(n)* What the government
imposes to protect the domestic
tobacco industry.

**tax** *(n)* What
government im-
poses to discourage
smoking.

**teenagers** *(n)* The only people left who still know that smoking is sophisticated.

**temptation** (*n*) Better you should
eat an apple.

**T.M.'s** *(n)* Tailor-mades.

**tobacco** *(n)* **1)** "Columbus
brought syphilis to the Indians,
and they gave him tobacco. It is
doubtful which is worse" (Harry
S Truman); **2)** "A lone man's
companion, a bachelor's friend, a
hungry man's food, a sad man's
cordial, a wakeful man's sleep,
and a chilly man's fire . . . there's
no herb like unto it under the
canopy of heaven" (Charles
Kingsley).

**tobacco industry** (n) The reason behind large sporting events.

**tongue** (n) The sort of food that will taste better when one quits.

**toothpaste/powder** (n) Walnut-stain stripper.

**ubiquitous** *(adj)* Non-smokers in the 1980s.

**United States** (*n*) A country in which in 1983: 52 million people smoked; 1.5 million smokers were seventeen or younger; 36 million people have quit since 1966; 3,494 cigarettes were smoked per person, or, 600 billion cigarettes were consumed; 36 states have laws restricting smoking; $866 million was spent on cigarette advertising; $25.8 million was lost to employers through smokers' absenteeism.

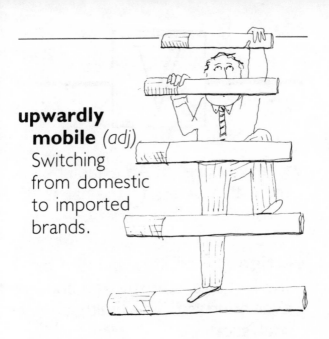

**upwardly mobile** *(adj)* Switching from domestic to imported brands.

**urge** *(n)* The prelude to a crave.

**useless** *(adj)* A half-smoked cigarette floating in a toilet.

**user-friendly** *(adj)* A nostalgic social attitude towards smokers.

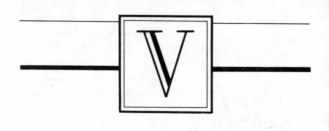

**variety store** *(n)* An establishment that caters to the habits of those who abhor variety.

**vertigo** *(n)* The state induced by the first cigarette smoked and ever after associated with sophistication.

**vicious circle** *(n)* See vicious circle.

**Virginia** (n) Mecca.

**Virginia Slims** (n) **1)** *Anorexia nicotina*; **2)** You've come the wrong way, baby.

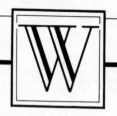

**warning** *(n)* 'Smoking can seriously damage your wealth.''

**washroom** *(n)* The smoking loges of the !980s.

**waste** *(n)* Any cigarette one lights at a bus stop.

**wave** *(n)* A familiar smoker's gesture to clear the air in any discussion with a non-smoker.

**weed** *(n)* **1)** Gardener's blight, smoker's delight; **2)** City in northern California.

**wheeze** *(n)* The noisy alien in one's chest.

**willpower** *(n)* Something smokers know they have and therefore don't have to prove.

**wimp** (n) Anyone who didn't quit when you did.

**withdrawal** (n) Physical symptoms may include hunger, constipation, perspiration, dizziness, increased cough, insomnia or sleepiness, sore scalp, and itchy hands and feet. Psychological symptoms may include tendency to depression, difficulty in con- centrating, irrita- bility, nervousness . . . all said symptoms arise from think- ing about quitting. See also Virginia.

**woman** (*n*) "And a woman is only a woman, but a good cigar is a smoke." (Rudyard Kipling)

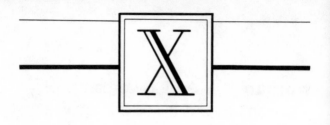

**x-ray** (*n*) A negative insight.

**xylophone** (*n*) An instrument for musicians with no wind.

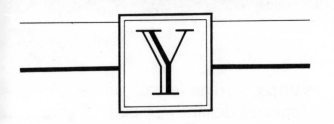

**yellow stains** *(n)* The antique gold finish on the fingers and teeth of a mature smoker.

**yoga** *(n)* Positions assumed, often involuntarily, by newly reform-ed smokers.

**yuppy** (*n*) The female of the species defiantly smokes (Camel Lights, Dunhills); the male gave up three years ago. Both occasionally "do" a little nostalgic dope.

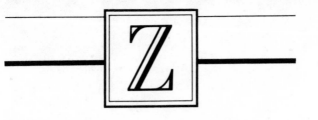

**zeitgeist** *(n)* Rather like tobacco, it's in one era and out the next.

**zero-hour** *(n)* No more ifs, ands, or butts.

THE END